Endorsements for *The Gospel Revisited*

I wholeheartedly endorse Aaron Bailey's new book "The Gospel Revisited". It is not only written very well, but simple enough for a child to understand and yet profound enough for a scholar to stop and rethink their premises. One of the foundational corner pieces of the early churches message was beauty. If the message we teach and live is not beautiful then it is not the gospel. Aaron does a phenomenal job revealing the beauty of the to good to be true news and I encourage everyone to read it and share it with as many people as possible.

Rev. Jamie Englehart
Overseer of the C.I.M. Network
Author of *Myths & Mistranslations*

In every generation, there is a need for fresh voices with fresh insight declaring "present truth." Aaron Bailey is such a voice—laboring to see the generations walk in truth. He is a leader in the Lord's Church with a passion to see all awakened to the great news of God's goodness.

In *The Gospel Revisited*, he skillfully leads us to look introspectively at what we may have believed about the gospel incorrectly. His desire is that we would be postured to take a new look. He guides us to "see" Christ, the Cross, and the Gospel with new eyes—eyes that awaken love, hope, acceptance, healing, and identity.

I was personally impacted by his fresh revelation of the Cross: "The Cross is God stepping into the worst we can do and answering with the best He can give." To this I say amen!

I wholeheartedly recommend this resource to all who seek to accurately share this "too good to be true" news with fresh perspective—offering hope, joy, healing, and the awakening of the relationship we have always longed for. It's time to return home for real.

Rev. Daryl O'Neil
Ruach Church Chicago
Barnabus Apostolic Alliance

In *The Gospel Revisited*, Aaron C. Bailey offers both the believer and the seeker a fresh vision of God's truth. He makes clear that God's love has never been interrupted or broken, no matter the circumstance, not in the garden, not on the cross, and not by our lives today. This book invites us to reimagine our relationship with a God whose love is unrelenting and whose grace is abundant. It also helps us to love one another better, because we come to see just how much God loves us.

Rev. Dr. James C. Bailey
Pastor, St. Stephen AME Church, Chicago, IL

Aaron Bailey's *The Gospel Revisited* is a breath of fresh grace. With clarity and insight, he reminds us that the good news isn't about fear, shame, or earning points with God—it's about discovering you already belong. Equal parts healing and wake-up call, this book dismantles toxic religion and unveils a Love too good to be anything less than God Himself. If you've ever wondered whether the Gospel could actually be good, Bailey's answer is a resounding—and life-changing—YES!

Dr. Matt Pandel
President, Global Grace Seminary
Theologian, Behavioral Psychologist, Educator

Aaron C. Bailey has written a wonderfully gracious, thoughtful, and impactful piece that warmly welcomes readers into God's Word and family. It offers the reader a renewed sense of God's loving presence, kindness, and faithfulness, regardless of who they are or what they have done. In a world that is constantly tossed around and destabilized by life's forces, this book helps readers clearly understand that God is crazy in love with them and that there is a place in God's heart and mind reserved just for them.

rev. cheryl l. green, phd.
Scholar, Activist, Womanist Theologian

"The word *gospel* means 'good news.' Jesus and his early followers had a proclamation of good news to make: God has not rejected you! He has made a way for you to know Him as a loving Father.

Jesus not only came to set us free from sin but also from religion—performing and striving to reach God. In fact,

Jesus came to radically transform our understanding of who God is. More than that, Jesus himself *is* the revelation of God. If you have seen Jesus, you have seen the Father.

I highly recommend Aaron's book, *The Gospel Revisited*. If all it does is cause you to pause and rethink some of your presumptions, it will have done a great job. Many Christians are afraid to rethink what they have been taught, but even the disciples had to rethink what *they* had been taught in order to embrace the Good News. The Good News is better than we have been told. God is better than we have been told. Jesus is the proof of that!"

Dr. Martin Trench
Pastor & Theologian
Author of *Eyes Wide Open*

Ask any Believer, 'What is the Gospel?' and you will hear a variety of answers. That alone reveals how desperately we need writings that return us to the center of our faith —works that not only inform but also unveil the very heart of God. In *The Gospel Revisited*, Aaron C. Bailey offers precisely that. With clarity, conviction, and grace, he provides an excellent example of what the Gospel truly is and why it matters—not only for our own lives, but for the world God so loves.

Rev. William Johnson
Senior Leader of Oxygen Church, Hilton Head, SC
Author of *The Prophetic Principle*

The Gospel Revisited is a rare gift to the Church—a breath of fresh air for the weary, disillusioned, and spiritually hungry. With clarity and compassion, Aaron C. Bailey peels back centuries of distortion and reintroduces the gospel not as information or transaction, but as the life-altering revelation of God's relentless love. This is not just a book to be read, but an invitation to be transformed. Written with the tenderness of a shepherd and the fire of a prophet, it points us to Jesus, who reveals a Father who has never been distant, reluctant, or anything less than love. I wholeheartedly recommend this book. It will renew your heart, deepen your faith, and awaken you to the beauty of the gospel you may have heard, but perhaps never truly seen.

Dr. Matthew Hester
Pastor of Dominion Church
Author of *The Rorschach God*

This book is a sacred and tender invitation—to draw near and *experience* the gospel not merely as belief, but as living relationship. Within these pages, the good news of Jesus Christ unfolds as the revelation of a love so pure, so unconditionally given, that it asks for nothing in return. God's love is a love that cannot be contained in words—only encountered, embodied, and lived.

Here, readers are gently invited into the transforming reality of a divine embrace—unceasing, unearned, and everlasting. This is the LOVE that was, is, and forever will be—the love humanity has always longed for, searching to fill a space that only God's love can fill.

Rev. Bailey invites us to step out of the shadows of shame, guilt, and striving, to lay down the exhausting need to be "enough," and to open the door to light—the light of grace and truth that has been shining within and around us all along.

With compassion and clarity, this book offers a path of liberation: beyond oppression, perfectionism, punishment, and religious performance—into the spacious freedom of mercy, grace, and agape love.

This is more than a message—it is an encounter. It is the call to awaken to who we already are: beloved, whole, and forever held in the eternal love of God.

Rev. Dr. Diane Bogues
Associate Dean of Students,
Iliff School of Theology

I believe Aaron has captured the breadth and beauty of the Gospel for such a time as this. *The Gospel Revisited* is a prophetic invitation to rediscover the "Good News" that first set our hearts and lives ablaze. As you read through these pages, you will sense the Spirit's breath on Aaron's words, calling us to the wholeness Jesus offers through His boundless grace.

Rev. Michelle Harding
Senior Leader, Church of The King, Easton, MD

Aaron C. Bailey has written the book many of us needed years ago—a grace-drenched, heartfelt vision of the gospel that refuses to weaponize Scripture or reduce God's love to a transaction. With pastoral warmth and careful theological insight, he gently unravels the fear-driven distortions that have wounded so many. He lovingly guides us back to the breathtaking reality at the heart of Christianity: we are already loved, already home, already held in the embrace of a God who has never stopped being for us! This is the kind of book that doesn't just inform—it's one that truly heals and restores.

Rev. Dr. Reginald Blount
Professor of Formation, Leadership, and Culture
Garrett-Evangelical Theological Seminary

The Gospel Revisited:
Recovering the Truth and Wonder of the Good News

Aaron C. Bailey

Eternum House Publishing
Chicago, Illinois

The Gospel Revisited: Recovering the Truth and Wonder of the Good News
© 2025 Aaron C. Bailey

Published by **Eternum House Publishing**, Chicago, Illinois.

Scripture References
Unless otherwise noted, Scripture quotations are taken from:

The Holy Bible, New International Version®, NIV®. Copyright © 1973, 1978, 1984, 2011 by Biblica, Inc.™ Used by permission. All rights reserved worldwide.

The Holy Bible, English Standard Version®, ESV®. Copyright © 2001 by Crossway Bibles, a publishing ministry of Good News Publishers. Used by permission. All rights reserved.

The Holy Bible, New Living Translation®, NLT®. Copyright © 1996, 2004, 2015 by Tyndale House Foundation. Used by permission. All rights reserved.

ISBN: 979-8-218-84498-1

Printed in the United States of America

Cover design by **Aaron C. Bailey**
Interior design by **Aaron C. Bailey**   ·

Dedication

For all who are searching and longing for more.
May you find the ancient, beautiful truth that has been waiting
for you all along: you have always been seen, you have always
been loved, you have always belonged.

Table of Contents

Author's Note

I wrote this book as an invitation — for the weary, the disillusioned, the seekers, and the skeptics. It's for anyone who has heard a version of the gospel that left them afraid, ashamed, or empty, and wondered if there was more. The good news is far better than we've been told. It's not only about avoiding hell or waiting for heaven; it's about union with God, wholeness, presence, and transformation — here and now.

My prayer is that these words awaken you to what has always been true: you are already loved, already held, already home. May you see and believe the beauty of the gospel, and may it free you to live in it fully — for His glory, and for the generations to come. And when you do, may your life become a living echo of that good news to everyone you meet.

Introduction

In a world oversaturated with noise, opinion, and half-truth, the Gospel often lies buried beneath cultural assumptions and religious tradition. To some, it has become a distant idea—at best, a ticket to heaven; at worst, a moral code.

But the Gospel is neither distant nor diminished. It is alive. It is present. It is glorious. Its origin is ancient, rooted in the very life and love of God Himself, yet it remains ever fresh, ever near, ever burning with relevance.

These are not new ideas. This is the faith once delivered to the saints. The message proclaimed by the apostles. The hope that carried the early Church through fire, empire, and persecution. It has outlasted kings. It has healed generations. It has never stopped transforming lives.

And now it comes to you.

It is time to search again: to peel back the layers of distortion and rediscover the Gospel that is actually good news—for you, for your neighbor, for the world.

What follows is not merely information. It is an invitation. An invitation to awaken. To remember. To return. To belong. To live.

Chapter One
What Gospel Did You Hear?

Most people would say they've heard the Gospel. They've heard it in Sunday school classrooms, revival meetings, social media posts, and dinner table debates. They've heard it shouted from pulpits, printed on tracts, and boiled down to slogans like "Turn or burn" or "Jesus died for your sins."

But let's pause.

What gospel did you hear?

Was it news so good it set your heart ablaze? Was it so compelling, so full of grace and truth, that you dropped your defenses and followed? Or was it fear dressed up in Scripture, shame cloaked in tradition, control disguised as moral performance?

The Apostle Paul raised the same alarm in his letter to the Galatians. Only a short time after believing, they were already being tugged toward a revised message—one tangled again in religious performance. He writes with urgency, "I am astonished that you are so quickly deserting the one who called you to live in the grace of Christ and are turning to a different gospel—which is really no gospel at all" (Galatians 1:6–7, NIV). From the very beginning, the Church had to discern between the authentic announcement of Christ and its counterfeits. Paul knew that when the gospel is altered, the image of God is blurred—and when our vision of God is blurred, our lives soon follow.

The truth is, many of us haven't heard the Gospel at all. We heard a bargain. We heard a threat. We heard a version so filtered through punishment and performance that we never truly met the God who is Love.

Some were handed a gospel of legalism: *God is holy, you are sinful, and Jesus died to absorb His wrath because He couldn't bear to look at you.* Salvation was presented as a transaction—God's anger appeased in exchange for your obedience. It sounded holy, but it was hollow. It left you serving a God you feared but didn't trust.

Others were offered a prosperity gospel—blessing without transformation, hope without repentance, inspiration without incarnation.

Still others were taught a nationalist gospel, draped in patriotic language that confused God's Kingdom with earthly power. Or an exclusive gospel, where only a chosen few belonged and the rest were disposable. Or a gospel of grit, where God's blessing was earned through relentless effort and His favor had to be kept through spiritual performance.

Different in tone, yet alike in one tragic way: none of them is the Gospel of Jesus Christ.

This cycle is not unique to our time. Across the centuries the message of Jesus has often been reshaped whenever it became entangled with power. In the fourth century, after Christianity was joined to imperial interests, the Gospel was recast to legitimize conquest. In the medieval West, it was frequently interpreted in the logic of debts and penalties, echoing the economic structures of the day. In every age, the temptation has been the same: to exchange the living announcement of God's mercy for a version that manages people and props up our systems.

"If the news you've heard has not made your heart burn with both relief and wonder, then you haven't yet heard the Gospel in its fullness."

These distortions didn't come out of nowhere. History shows us that whenever the Church became tangled with empire, culture, or fear of losing control, the message shifted. We borrowed the language of Rome's courts, the incentives of the marketplace, or the hierarchies of our own society—and soon we were preaching something easier to manage than the wild, world-turning, "almost too good to be true" news of the Kingdom.

But the real Gospel is not about escaping the world—it is about being transformed within it. It is not about earning favor, but awakening to the favor you already have. It is not about fear, shame, or endless striving—it is about the scandalous goodness of a God who refuses to be distant.

Even the word "gospel" carried subversive weight in the first-century. *Euangelion* was the empire's vocabulary for "good news"—the birth of a new emperor, a military victory, the promise of peace through Rome's strength. When the apostles took that word on their lips, they turned it inside out. The good news they preached was not domination but deliverance, not the sword but the cross, not allegiance to Caesar but the kingship of Jesus. To confess "Jesus is Lord" was to say, "Caesar is not." Their message was not private advice for the soul; it was a public announcement that a new reign had begun.

The real Gospel does not wait on the far side of a chasm for you to climb across. It walks toward you in the dust of your shame, speaking life into places you thought were beyond redemption.

Think of the woman in Samaria, drawing water at noon when the streets were empty. Her neighbors had judged her; her past had marked her; her present was lonely. Into that moment walked Jesus—ignoring every cultural, religious, and gender boundary that said He shouldn't speak to her. He didn't begin with condemnation. He began with thirst: "Will you give Me a drink?"

She came for water. He came to reveal Living Water. By the time she left, she was no longer defined by shame. She ran back to the very people who had rejected her, declaring, *"Come, see a man who told me everything I ever did—and loved me still."*

This is the texture of the true gospel: it disarms humiliation and restores dignity. Counterfeit versions do the opposite. They multiply guilt, cultivate fear, and keep people on a treadmill of proving they belong. Jesus does not traffic in exploitation of our failures. He names the truth and then names us beloved. Notice what happens to her story—she, who once avoided the crowd goes looking for them. The encounter that exposed her past also opened her future. When the real gospel is heard, heads lift, hearts soften, and people run with a testimony instead of hiding in self-contempt.

That is what it feels like when the Gospel is truly heard. It doesn't just correct your doctrine; it restores your dignity. It reorders how you see God, yourself, and the world.

The Gospel is not an offer—it is a declaration. It is the unveiling of a reality already set in motion. Jesus didn't come to persuade the Father to love you; He came to reveal the love the Father has always had for you. He didn't come to start a religion, but to reveal a relationship.

God is like Jesus. Exactly like Jesus. He has always been like Jesus. We didn't always know this, but now we do.

And that changes everything.

If God has always looked like Jesus, why do so many of us still live as though He were distant or hard to reach? Why do our prayers sometimes sound like we are trying to convince a reluctant God to draw near? The problem is not that God has withdrawn. The tragedy is that we believed a lie— that distance is real. And that is the very illusion we will confront next.

If the news you've heard has not made your heart burn with both relief and wonder, then you haven't yet heard the Gospel in its fullness. So let us hear it again—this time, with unveiled hearts.

Chapter Two
The Real Problem: Separation

Every great tragedy begins with a lie. And one of the most destructive lies whispered into the human heart is this: *You are far from God.*

It rarely comes shouted from pulpits. More often, it slips quietly into our thinking, cloaked in religious language:

"God can't look on sin."
"Your sins have separated you from Him."
"Get right with God before it's too late."

But what if the real problem isn't distance at all? What if the separation we've been taught to fear is not reality, but illusion?

Many of us were handed verses like proof-texts to prove God had pulled away from us. One of the most common is Isaiah 59:2:

> *"Your iniquities have separated you from your God; your sins have hidden his face from you so that he will not hear"* (NIV).

For years, that verse was preached as if it meant God abandoned sinners. But if we read Isaiah 59 in full, we find the prophet describing Israel's perception of estrangement, not God's actual withdrawal. The chapter begins, *"Surely the arm of the Lord is not too short to save, nor his ear too dull to hear"* (Isaiah 59:1). The problem was never God's absence—it was the people's blindness, their inability to see that God was still near.

The New Testament makes this even clearer. Paul tells the Colossians that we were once *"alienated and enemies in our minds because of wicked works"* (Colossians 1:21, NKJV). Notice carefully: the alienation was "in our minds." It was a felt distance, not an actual one. Humanity turned inward, convinced of separation, yet God never abandoned His creation. He was always moving toward us, not away.

Listen again to the first story. The garden is heavy with the scent of fruit. The sun slants low. A man and a woman hide among the trees. Their breath is shallow. Their hearts pound—not from running, but from shame.

Then—footsteps. The sound of the Voice that formed them. Not in a storm of judgment, but walking in the cool of the day. Not demanding their return, but asking, "Where are you?"

It is not the cry of an offended deity. It is the call of a Father seeking His children. From the very beginning, God's first response to human failure was not withdrawal—it was pursuit.

This is the rhythm of the biblical story: we hide, and God comes looking. We run, and He follows. We resist, and He remains.

Yet we've been told another story—that God's holiness demands distance, that His presence is reserved for the sinless. But Scripture gives us another picture entirely. He traveled with Israel through the wilderness, His glory filling the tabernacle in the midst of their grumbling (Exodus 40:34–38). He pledged Himself to Israel through unfaithfulness, like a husband who refuses to walk away (Hosea 2:14–20). He stepped into the fire with three Hebrew boys in Babylon (Daniel 3:24–27). He found Jonah in the sea's depths, breathing mercy into a runaway prophet (Jonah 2:1–10). He entered the womb of a teenage girl under Roman occupation (Luke 1:26–38). He hung between criminals, speaking forgiveness into the air thick with mockery (Luke 23:32–34).

God has never been afraid of our condition.

The Apostle Paul wrote that we were once "alienated in our minds" (Colossians 1:21). He wasn't describing a cosmic gap. He was naming a fog in our thinking—a false consciousness that made us believe God had withdrawn. The distance was never ontological; it was psychological, imagined. We were lost in the dark not because He left, but because we forgot where the light was.

The earliest voices of the Church echoed this same truth. Athanasius, in *On the Incarnation*, insisted that God did not retreat from the world after sin but drew even closer, taking on our very flesh so that "He might turn again the corruptible to incorruption." Irenaeus spoke of humanity's fall not as the loss of God's presence but as a kind of forgetfulness. Sin, he said, is amnesia of the Father's love, and Christ comes as the reminder— recapitulating the whole human story so that what was lost in Adam is gathered up in Him.

From the Scriptures to the Fathers, the testimony is clear: the separation was never on God's side. It was a wound in our sight, a blindness of the heart.

"The Cross does not solve the problem of God's absence. It reveals the truth of His presence."

So we built altars to summon Him, not realizing we were already dwelling within His presence.

That is why the Gospel does not summon a distant deity—it awakens us to a very present Christ. The ache you feel for God is not the longing of an orphan; it is the hunger of a child already home, learning again the sound of the Father's voice.

Even your longing is proof of union. The very desire for Him is the echo of His presence within you. Every step you've taken—toward Him or away—has been inside the circle of His nearness.

This is why Paul could proclaim with such boldness, *"God was in Christ reconciling the world to Himself, not counting their trespasses against them"* (2 Corinthians 5:19, ESV). Notice the language—God was not distant, waiting for the Cross to soften His heart. He was in Christ, present in the suffering, refusing to abandon us even at our worst. The Cross does not solve the problem of God's absence; it unveils the reality of His presence.

What changes at Calvary is not God's posture toward us but our perception of Him. At the Cross the lie of abandonment is shattered. We discover that even when we do our worst—mocking, rejecting, crucifying—the Father does not withdraw. He absorbs the blow and answers with forgiveness.

When we believe the myth of separation, we live like orphans, forever hustling for belonging. When we awaken to union, we live like children at home—secure, seen, and safe in the Father's embrace. Jesus did not die to change the Father's mind about us; He died to open our eyes to the Father's heart toward us.

In Him we live and move and have our being. We are enfolded in His life, even when our vision is blurred.

So let this sink in: you have never been outside His reach. You have never been beyond His touch. You have never taken a breath apart from His sustaining presence. The only distance that exists is the one we imagine.

And the Gospel? It is the Voice still walking through the gardens of our shame, calling into every hiding place: *"Where are you?"*

Not because He can't see us—but because we've forgotten where He's always been.

Chapter Three
The Lie That Changed Everything

I t began in the garden, under the heavy air of a day untouched by rain. The ground still held the warmth of the morning sun. Leaves whispered overhead as a presence, unseen yet familiar, moved through the air.

And then—another voice.

Not loud. Not harsh. But coiled in softness: *"Did God really say...?"* (Genesis 3:1).

The question was not about fruit alone. It was about trust—about the very nature of the One who had formed them. Beneath the words lay a deeper suggestion: *God is holding out on you.*

The serpent didn't need to overpower them. He only needed to shift their vision. If mistrust could take root, the rest would follow.

The woman hesitated. She repeated what she thought she knew of God's words, but the seed of doubt was already there. She looked again at the fruit. It was pleasing. It was desirable. It was within reach.

The bite was only the symptom. The real break had already happened—in the moment she began to see God through the lens of lack.

This is where the lie entered the human story: not that we are bad and God is good, but that God's goodness is questionable. That He withholds. That He is like us—frail, self-protective, quick to withdraw when disappointed.

But God's holiness is not an improved version of human decency. It is altogether other—separate in kind, not just degree. His love is not fragile. His awareness is not limited. His goodness is not calculating.

The story of Eden was not told in a vacuum. Israel's neighbors had their own accounts of beginnings—tales where the gods were volatile, suspicious, and self-serving. In Mesopotamian myths, humanity was often created as slaves, existing only to satisfy divine whims. In these stories, the gods guarded their power jealously, striking humans down for daring to step out of line.

Against this backdrop, Genesis is startling. Here is a God who creates not from violence but from love, who breathes His own life into humanity, who walks with His children in the cool of the day. Here is a God who entrusts creation to human hands and withholds nothing essential.

It is into this generous world that the serpent's voice slithers. His words carry the same suspicion that defined the pagan imagination: *God is holding out on you. He cannot be trusted. His commands are not for your good, but for His own gain.* The serpent does not invent a new lie; he borrows an old one, importing into the garden the distorted vision of divinity that surrounded Israel.

The bite of the fruit was not the first sin. The first sin was a shift in sight—the moment they began to imagine God as one of those capricious deities, calculating and untrustworthy. They traded the vision of a Father with open hands for the caricature of a god with clenched fists.

The tragedy was never the bite. It was the belief that God could not be trusted—a belief born from seeing Him through our own frailty rather than His holiness.

The consequence of mistrust did not stop in that garden. It rippled outward into every relationship, every community, every system humanity would ever build. What began as a private suspicion became the seed of rivalry, blame, and violence. Adam turns against Eve: *"The woman you gave me..."* (Genesis 3:12). Their sons reenact the fracture in blood as Cain rises against Abel (Genesis 4:8). From that moment forward, human culture has been shaped as much by fear and competition, as by cooperation and trust.

The lie becomes the logic of empire: if God is withholding, then we must grasp, dominate, and control before someone else does. It becomes the soil of religion: if God cannot be trusted, then He must be appeased with sacrifices, rituals, and endless striving. It becomes the script of society: the strong rule the weak, suspicion trumps generosity, and violence masquerades as order.

This is why the story of Eden is not simply about one man and one woman long ago. It is the story of us all. Every system we inherit and every structure we build still bears the echo of that original distortion: God cannot be trusted, so we must secure life for ourselves.

Shame followed quickly. They covered themselves (Genesis 3:7). They hid among the trees

(Genesis 3:8). The sound of His approach, once their joy, now made them shrink.

But here is where the story turns. God did not thunder from the heavens. He walked. He called: *"Where are you?"*(Genesis 3:9).

This was not the cry of a furious judge. It was the seeking voice of a Father whose children had believed a lie about Him.

The earliest voices of the Church heard the story the same way. Irenaeus, writing in the second century, did not describe humanity as depraved beyond repair but as immature children who had been deceived. For him, sin was less rebellion than forgetfulness—amnesia of the Father's goodness. The serpent exploited that immaturity, and humanity lost sight of the God who had never lost sight of them.

Athanasius, in *On the Incarnation*, carried the thought forward. He insisted that God did not retreat from a fallen world but drew nearer, taking on our very flesh, so that, in his words, "He might turn again the corruptible to incorruption." The Incarnation was not damage control; it was God's eternal intention unveiled in time—the love that had always pursued us now clothed in human form.

From Scripture to the Fathers, the testimony is consistent: the separation was never on God's side. The breach was in our sight, not in His presence.

And the rest of the human story has played out in this pattern: the lie of separation leading us to hide, to strive, to build systems of religion and control—all in an effort to win back a nearness we never truly lost. We project our fears and limitations onto God and then live as though they are true.

I know this pattern well.

What we believe about God never stays private. It inevitably takes shape in the way we live, the way we build communities, and the way we lead others. A distorted vision of God produces distorted patterns in us. If we see Him as harsh, we will create harsh cultures. If we imagine Him as distant, our worship will carry distance. If we think He is quick to condemn, we will soon condemn in His name.

But when we see Him as He truly is— gracious, steadfast, abounding in love—something else begins to happen. We are transformed into the same image we behold (2 Corinthians 3:18). Communities formed by this vision become places of mercy, healing, and restoration. Leaders who live from this revelation learn to guide not by fear but by grace, not by control but by love.

This is why the lie in the garden matters so much. It was never just about fruit; it was about the image of God impressed on the human soul. Whatever vision of God you carry will be the vision that shapes your own reflection to the world.

The vision of God you hold will always surface, no matter how well you try to disguise it. It shows up in the tone of your prayers, the way you treat strangers, the culture you build in your home, the expectations you place on yourself, and even the way you handle failure. You cannot long pretend to believe in a gracious God while living out of fear, nor can you truly believe in a condemning God and still embody mercy. In time, the God you imagine will be the God you mirror.

For years, I believed in the love of God—at least in theory. I could preach it, quote it, and sing about it. But I didn't know it in its depth. It had not yet permeated my core, healed my wounds, or brought me into a wholeness visible in the rhythms of my life.

I knew how to be polite in church culture. I was kind to those who were kind to me. But if someone crossed me, I could play the long game of silent offense. I knew how to walk alongside others with a firm hand—sometimes more human effort than Spirit-led grace—driven by ambition and by my own vision of what a "disciple of Aaron Bailey" should look like. Too much kindness seemed like weakness. Too much love felt unnecessary. I embraced a kind of "apostolic aggression" that was more performance than truth—and if I'm honest, it was never truly me.

Then came the moment that stopped me. Someone I had been walking alongside told me why he had hidden certain struggles from me: *"Because you're not safe."*

I was shocked. I thought I was approachable. But in truth, if you disappointed me too much, I worried more about how it reflected on me, than how it wounded you. That had nothing to do with the heart of God.

Over the last decade, God has undone that version of me. Through seasons of obscurity, brokenness, growth, and word after word about it being my time to be "hidden," I have come to understand that God was not punishing me; He was healing me. He was making me whole, teaching me to lead with love, stripping me of all traces of personal ambition, and perfecting me for what He called me to do.

The wilderness was not wasted. It was where I learned that His presence is the making place for prophets and leaders (Hosea 2:14–15). In His presence, I was changed—not remade into someone else, but revealed as who I had always been in the mind of God (Ephesians 1:4–5).

Christ in me—the hope of glory (Colossians 1:27)—was no longer a theological idea but a lived reality. I was healed in places I didn't know were broken, made whole in ways I could never have orchestrated.

And as my belief in the absolute goodness of God expanded, so did I. Perfectionism crumbled under grace. Surface-level "church nice" gave way to Christ being formed in me (Galatians 4:19).

With that came clarity about my calling. I even went back to the person I had once been discipling—not to reopen old wounds, but to honor the healing by seeking his blessing. I did not want to offer wholeness to others without first making right what had been broken.

When I began to believe that His goodness was not like mine at all, but wholly other, it changed the way I lead, the way I listen, the way I forgive, the way I wait.

So the question is not simply, *Do I believe in God?* It is this: *Do I believe He is as good as He says He is?*

Because the truest thing about you is not what you've done or what's been done to you. The truest thing about you is who you are in the eyes of a God who has only ever been love (1 John 4:8–10). And the moment you believe that, everything changes.

If the lie in the garden distorted our vision of God, then the only cure is God's own unveiling. That is why the story does not end with our suspicion but with His self-revelation. Left to ourselves, we project our fears onto the heavens and call them holy. But in Jesus, God interrupts the cycle. He is not simply another prophet pointing toward God: He is what God has to say. In Him, the invisible becomes visible, the distant becomes near, and the questioned goodness of God stands revealed without shadow or condition.

Chapter Four
Jesus Is What God Has to Say

I f you miss this, you miss the heart of the Gospel: Jesus is exactly what God is like. Not part of Him. Not the "nice" side. Not a temporary display of compassion before the Father's "real" nature returns. He is the perfect revelation of who God has always been (John 1:14; Colossians 1:15; Hebrews 1:3).

John opens his Gospel with thunderous simplicity:

> *"No one has ever seen God; the only begotten Son, who is close to the Father's heart, has made Him known"* (John 1:18).

The Greek word for *"made Him known"* is *exēgēsato*—the root of our word *exegesis*. Jesus is the exegesis of God. He is the interpretation of the unseen Father. Everything the world has ever misunderstood about God finds its correction, not in a new law or philosophy, but in a person.

The writer of Hebrews continues the thought: *"He is the radiance of God's glory and the exact representation of His being"* (Hebrews 1:3). The Son is not a dim reflection or a partial glimpse; He is the perfect expression of divine reality. When we look at Jesus forgiving, healing, eating with sinners, or blessing the broken, we are not witnessing God momentarily softening His tone. We are seeing the eternal character of God unveiled.

Jesus does not stand between us and an irritable deity, convincing the Father to be merciful. He stands within the Father, revealing that mercy was the heartbeat of God all along. He is not the gentle side of God; He is God made visible. To see Him is to see the Father's face without distortion or disguise.

Why does this matter? Because until we believe it, we will continue to live with a divided vision—loving Jesus while quietly fearing the Father, trusting His mercy, but suspecting His motives. We will project our own harshness, our own conditional love, onto heaven and call it holiness.

Long before Bethlehem, the same God was revealing His heart. Moses glimpsed it on Sinai when the Lord passed before him and declared, *"The Lord, the Lord, compassionate and gracious, slow to anger, abounding in love and faithfulness"* (Exodus 34:6). Isaiah saw it in his vision of the temple, when holiness filled the air not as a threat but as glory that cleansed a trembling prophet (Isaiah 6:1–7). David sang of it again and again: *"The Lord is gracious and compassionate, slow to anger and rich in love"* (Psalm 145:8).

All of these were early brushstrokes on the same canvas. What was hinted at in shadow finds its full color in Christ. The mercy that covered Adam, the patience that carried Israel, the presence that filled the temple—all converge in Jesus. He is not God changing His tone; He is God showing His face.

When Jesus tells Philip, *"Whoever has seen Me has seen the Father"* (John 14:9), He is not offering a poetic metaphor. He is declaring that the search is over. The holiness that once terrified now takes you by the hand. The glory that dwelt behind a veil now looks at you and smiles.

If God has always been like Jesus, then every shadow you've feared in His face was never truly there.

The earliest theologians of the Church guarded this truth as the cornerstone of our faith. Gregory of Nyssa wrote that "in the Son, the Father is seen," and that to look upon Jesus is to behold "the beauty of the invisible nature." Tertullian declared that "the Son is the Word through whom the Father is made known," meaning that Christ is not a momentary expression of divine mercy but the ongoing language of God's being.

Athanasius would later write that "the Word of God became man so that we might learn the nature of the Father," emphasizing that the Incarnation was revelation, not rescue alone. Jesus did not come to change God's mind about humanity; He came to change humanity's mind about God.

For the early Church, this was not a poetic flourish—it was the essence of orthodoxy. To know Jesus was to know God as He truly is: unchanging in love, unwavering in goodness, and endlessly near. This has always been the confession of the Church, even when our practice has failed to mirror it.

The Gospels do not present Jesus as a partial portrait. He is the Word made flesh: God's message in human skin. He is the visible image of the invisible God. He is the exact imprint of God's being.

That means when Jesus heals the leper by touching him before cleansing him (Mark 1:40–42), we are seeing exactly how God responds to the untouchable: not with recoil, but with embrace.

When He shields the woman caught in adultery from her accusers and restores her dignity (John 8:1–11), we see exactly how God deals with our shame: not by adding to it, but by lifting it.

When He prays for those crucifying Him, *"Father, forgive them, for they know not what they do"* (Luke 23:34), we hear exactly how God speaks over our worst violence and rejection: not with vengeance, but with mercy.

Jesus is not a softer side of God. He is God—unfiltered, unveiled, unchanging.

If you want a picture of the Father's heart, watch the story Jesus tells of a wayward son (Luke 15:11–32). The boy had left home, squandered his inheritance, and returned filthy, rehearsing an apology he hoped would earn him a servant's place. But the father—already watching for him—ran down the road to meet him. He threw his arms around him before a single excuse could be offered. He clothed him, restored him, and threw a feast.

Jesus didn't tell that story to make us wish the Father were that kind. He told it because the Father *is* that kind. The running, embracing, restoring father in the parable is not a metaphor for a momentary mood—it is a mirror of the eternal heart of God.

This is why seeing Jesus clearly is more than theological correctness. It is a lens that reshapes the way we live and love.

When the Christ you see is the Christ who truly is, the distance between you and the Father collapses—not because He moved, but because your eyes finally opened.

It changes how you pray—you no longer plead with a reluctant God; you commune with a willing Friend.

It changes how you lead—you no longer motivate with fear; you draw people with love.

It changes how you forgive—you no longer hold grudges as leverage; you release them as worship.

It changes how you see yourself—you no longer measure your worth by performance; you rest in belovedness (John 15:9).

Look at Jesus. That is the whole message. Every healing, every meal, every tear, every laugh, every scar, they are all God speaking, without stutter or shadow. And He is still speaking.

And yet, many still live as though Jesus and the Father are of two minds. We speak of grace but move through life like servants afraid of a master's mood. We pray as if we must convince God to be good, worship as if He might withdraw, and minister as if we must earn what has already been given.

The Gospel reveals something far different: there has never been a moment when the Father and the Son were at odds. The mercy we see in Jesus is the mercy that has always burned in the Father's heart. The cross did not create that love: it exposed it.

When this truth begins to take root, striving gives way to trust. Fear yields to friendship. Prayer becomes conversation instead of negotiation. We stop living to win God's approval, and start living from His affection. The same Spirit that rested on Jesus now rests in us, whispering the same affirmation: *"You are My beloved."*

This is the invitation of union: to live as those already included, already loved, already home.

When we begin to see God this way, the Gospel itself starts to sound new—yet it is the oldest truth in existence. The story was never about an angry deity who needed to be appeased, but about a loving Father making Himself known. Jesus does not revise the message; He reveals it. He shows us that what we call "good news" is not an escape plan for sinners but the unveiling of a Kingdom already breaking in.

If God has always been like Jesus, then everything we believe about salvation, justice, and restoration must be retold in that light. The Gospel must be revisited: not to add to it, but to finally see it as it really is. This is where we go next: to hear the good news again, this time through the eyes of the One who is Himself the message.

Chapter Five
The Cross Was Not Plan B

Many of us were handed a gospel built around emergency. We were taught that sin caught God off guard, that humanity's fall forced heaven into crisis, and that the Cross was God's last-ditch effort to salvage a broken plan. As if Eden failed. As if creation was a gamble. As if Jesus was a reaction instead of a revelation.

But love doesn't improvise. It incarnates.

The Cross was never Plan B.

Before there was sin, there was the Lamb slain from the foundation of the world (Revelation 13:8).

Before Adam reached for the fruit, the Father had already chosen union. Before humanity ever said "no," heaven had already said "yes." The Cross was not the moment God figured out what to do with us. It was the moment we saw how far He had always been willing to go.

We must unlearn the idea that God required blood to be appeased—that a violent death was the only way to satisfy divine wrath; that the Father demanded torture to be reconciled. These ideas did not originate in the heart of God. They came from systems of religion that mirrored human empires more than divine compassion. Systems that believed peace could only be achieved through punishment. That forgiveness had to be purchased.

But Jesus did not come to pay off the Father. He came to reveal the Father. This is why when Jesus steps onto the scene, His first words are not about appeasing wrath but about awakening hearts.

When Jesus first begins His public ministry, He does not launch a new religion. He doesn't offer a sales pitch, a moral checklist, or a fear-driven warning. He steps into Galilee with a single, audacious announcement:

> *"The time is fulfilled, and the kingdom of God has come near; repent, and believe the good news"* (Mark 1:14–15).

For many of us, those words were framed as a threat: repent or else. But in Jesus' mouth, they were a declaration of arrival. The kingdom is here. The delay is over. The world you longed for is already breaking in.

The Greek word for "repent" is *metanoeō*, which means "to change one's mind" or "to think differently afterward." Jesus isn't demanding guilt; He is inviting awakening. He is saying, "Change the way you see everything—especially the way you see God." The call to repent is not a summons to self-loathing but an invitation to new perception.

The good news He proclaims is not about escaping this world but about discovering that God has stepped into it. The message is not, "Get to

45

heaven when you die," but, "Heaven's reality is drawing near to you now." Jesus stands as the living announcement that God's reign has already begun—where mercy rules instead of merit, and love outlasts judgment.

To hear the Gospel rightly, we must hear it as those first listeners did: as the shocking news that God is better than we imagined and closer than we believed.

Paul would later distill this same message into a single, world-shattering sentence: *"God was in Christ reconciling the world to Himself, not counting their trespasses against them"* (2 Corinthians 5:19). Those words dismantle every idea of distance, division, and negotiation. God was not outside of Christ, watching the crucifixion from a safe distance, deciding whether to forgive. He was inside it, entering the worst of our violence and shame to reveal a love that cannot be driven away.

The Cross, then, is not a transaction between an angry Father and a pleading Son. It is the self-giving act of the Triune God, Father, Son, and Spirit, absorbing our hostility and answering it with mercy. Reconciliation is not a deal to be struck, but a reality already accomplished. The blood does not purchase the Father's affection; it exposes it.

Paul's announcement means that salvation is not humanity convincing God to return to us but humanity awakening to the God who never left. The "world" God reconciled includes every person, every corner of creation. The invitation of the Gospel is simply to wake up to what is already true in Him.

This is why the early believers spoke of the Cross as revelation, not appeasement. It is God's great unveiling—Love standing in the open, arms outstretched, saying, *This is who I have always been.*

"Jesus did not die to change the Father's mind about us. He died to open our eyes to the Father's heart toward us."

At the Cross, we do not see a good Son shielding us from a cruel Father; we see the whole of the Godhead united in self-giving love. The Father was not absent. The Spirit was not silent. God was in Christ: participating in our pain, not punishing through it. Calvary was the moment heaven's heart was revealed, not divided.

When Jesus and His followers began to speak of *good news*, they were not coining a new religious slogan. The word *euangelion* already carried weight in the Roman world. It was the empire's language for victory and control. When a new emperor took the throne, heralds were sent throughout the provinces announcing *"good news"*—the *euangelion* of Caesar. It meant that Rome's power had prevailed, that peace would be maintained by the sword, that allegiance must now be given to the new ruler.

Into that atmosphere Jesus dared to use the same word. His *good news* was a holy rebellion against the propaganda of empire. He announced a kingdom without domination, a reign without coercion, a peace that did not depend on violence. The Gospel of Jesus is the subversion of every empire built on fear.

The early Christians understood this. To confess *"Jesus is Lord"* was to say *"Caesar is not."* It was not a private spiritual statement but a public declaration of a new reality: love had become the highest authority. The Gospel is not advice for better living or an offer of personal improvement: it is the royal announcement that another world has already begun, and that its King rules by self-giving love.

Jesus' death is not transactional; it is transformational. It does not change God's heart toward humanity. It reveals it. The Cross is not the moment God starts loving us. It is the moment we finally see how deep that love has always gone.

He took on our violence, our shame, our systems of death, and absorbed them into Himself, not to appease a cosmic scale, but to end the cycle of retribution once and for all. He drank the full cup of human cruelty and responded with, *"Father, forgive them"* (Luke 23:34). That is what love does. It suffers without resentment. It dies without revenge. It resurrects without punishment.

The Cross is God stepping into the worst we can do and answering with the best He can give. If this is how God operates, it reshapes our own response to wrongdoing. We can no longer justify retribution as righteousness. Instead, we are called to move toward restoration in all things, even when it may cost us. Forgive before the apology. Absorb the offense without allowing bitterness to take root (Romans 12:17–21).

The Cross calls us to live cruciform lives—not in morbid self-denial, but in love that gives itself away.

The Cross is not the center of the Gospel because God needed blood. It is the center because we needed to see Love laid bare. We needed to be undone by the sight of mercy refusing to strike back. We needed to behold a God who would rather die than be separated from His children: who would rather stretch out His arms than tighten His fist.

This is not weakness. This is glory.

A glory that does not come through conquest, but through other-centered love. A glory that refuses to meet violence with violence. A glory that turns the ugliest instrument of torture into the greatest sign of hope.

What Jesus reveals on the Cross is not a different version of God. He reveals that this has always been the way of God: sacrificial, forgiving, non-retaliatory love. Not just for the righteous. Not just for the repentant. But while we were still sinners, still enemies in our minds, still lost in the fog of separation (Romans 5:8–10).

He bore our sin: not because the Father couldn't look at it, but because He wanted us to see that He already had. Jesus doesn't shield us from God. He opens our eyes to God. And what do we see?

Not wrath.
Not vengeance.
Not fury.

We see a broken body and outstretched arms.

51

We see a God who doesn't demand sacrifice, but becomes it.

We see love, bloody and bruised, yet undefeated.

We see the end of all accusation.

We see the beginning of new creation.

The Cross was not Plan B. It was the eternal Yes.

The Yes that echoed before time.

The Yes that exposed every lie.

The Yes that answered every question.

The Yes that still speaks.

This is the Gospel: God has never stopped saying yes.

When we see the Cross this way, salvation stops being a rescue from God and becomes an awakening to God. The Gospel is not about escaping wrath; it is about discovering that Love Himself has stepped inside our story and made it His own. Redemption is not distance closed by effort but union unveiled by grace. The same life that conquered death now lives within us, drawing us into the communion that has always existed within the Father, Son, and Spirit. This is where the story turns again—from what Christ has done for us to what He is now doing within us.

Chapter Six
Atonement and Union

A tonement is not a bargaining table. It is not a tense meeting where God sits across from humanity, waiting to be persuaded to love us again. The Cross was not a transaction to calm divine anger. It was the unveiling of the love that never left.

In many churches, the word *atonement* is introduced like a legal term. The dominant picture is penal: God's justice demanding payment, humanity in debt, and Jesus standing in as our substitute to settle the account. For centuries this legal framework has shaped sermons, hymns, and hearts. And while it seeks to honor the seriousness of sin, it distorts the character of God if it paints Him as unwilling to forgive without first spilling blood.

Even so, the Church's imagination has often swung between these two pictures—courtroom and communion, transaction and transformation. Yet, through every era, the Spirit has kept a witness alive. Whenever believers rediscovered the language of participation, the Gospel sounded like good news again: the Holy One entering our estrangement until nothing was left outside His embrace.

Christians have wrestled with the meaning of atonement since the earliest days of the Church. In the West, the legal or penal view eventually became dominant—picturing Jesus as the one who satisfies the demands of law or wrath. But this was never the only way believers understood the Cross. In the second century, Irenaeus spoke of *recapitulation*— Christ entering every stage of human life to restore it to God. In the fourth century, Athanasius declared that the Son took on our humanity "that we might become partakers of His divinity." In the Eastern tradition, many spoke of *Christus Victor:* the victory of love over sin, death, and the devil. Across these diverse voices, one truth rang out: the Cross was never about God changing His mind about us. It was about God showing us that union and belonging were always His intention.

The first believers described atonement in ways that were relational, restorative, and victorious. The very word itself, "at-one-ment," points not to settling a score, but to bringing what is estranged into perfect harmony. This is why the New Testament never presents the Cross as God finally deciding to draw near, but as the moment when we see clearly that He always has been.

> *"You are not trying to become one with God. You are learning to live from the oneness you already have."*

Union with God was not achieved at Calvary. It was revealed there. The Cross did not build a bridge across an actual gulf in God's heart. Instead, it tore away the veil from our minds: the veil that had convinced us we were alone. This is why Paul writes, *"God was in Christ reconciling the world to Himself"* (2 Corinthians 5:19). Not reconciling Himself to the world, as if He were the one who needed convincing.

From the beginning, union was His intention. Eden opened with it. Israel's tabernacle and temple practices pointed to it. The psalmists sang of it. The prophets declared it. And on the night before His death, Jesus prayed not for us to try harder, but for us to live in the reality He had already given:

> *"I have given them the glory You gave Me, so they may be one as We are one—I in them and You in Me—that they may be perfected in unity"*
> (John 17:22–23).

The prayer of Jesus in John 17 is not a wish but a window. He is not asking the Father to make something new; He is unveiling what has always been true. "I in them, and You in Me," He said— words that hold the whole Gospel in one breath. The Cross did not create union; it unveiled it. The Incarnation showed us that God was never distant, never divided from His creation. In Christ, heaven and earth were already joined, and the veil that seemed to separate them was only in our minds. Paul would later echo this mystery: "Your life is hidden with Christ in God" (Colossians 3:3). The Cross did not purchase God's presence; it exposed the illusion of its absence. When Jesus prayed for oneness, He invited us into awareness, not striving, to awaken to the communion we were made for and have never truly lost.

Picture that moment. The room dimly lit by oil lamps. The weight of betrayal hanging in the air. The disciples confused and restless. And Jesus, steady, looking past the Cross into the future, into your face, praying that you would know you are one with Him, even as He is one with the Father.

That prayer was not wishful thinking. It was the declaration of what His life and death would unveil. When the temple veil tore from top to bottom (Matthew 27:51), it was not God finally opening the door. It was God showing the door had never been locked.

Atonement, then, is not God deciding to love you after all. It is the unveiling of the truth that you were never outside His embrace. You are not trying to become one with God. You are learning to live from the oneness you already have. And that changes everything.

If you believe reconciliation is a contract, you will live like an employee—afraid to breach the terms. But if you believe reconciliation is your eternal reality, you will live like a child at home. You will pray differently: not auditioning for His attention, but speaking with One who shares your breath. You will forgive differently: not calculating debts, but releasing others into the same grace that holds you. You will see yourself differently: not as a sinner barely tolerated, but as the beloved in whom God delights. When you live this way, you begin to notice that union is not only personal but universal —the same grace breathing through you is holding everything together.

The Cross is the great unveiling. It is the moment when the lie of separation finally collapses under the weight of perfect love. And in that unveiling, you discover what has always been true: you are at one with the God who has only ever been for you.

Chapter Seven
The Resurrection Is the Revolution

If the resurrection is true, then everything changes. The earliest believers understood this so vividly, that resurrection became their entire worldview. To them, it was not a metaphor for hope but the arrival of a new world order. Paul called Christ the "first fruits" of those who have fallen asleep (1 Corinthians 15:20): language every farmer in the ancient world knew. The first fruit meant the harvest had begun; the future was already breaking into the present.

Resurrection wasn't simply Jesus' victory over death; it was *our* invitation to live from the future reality that had already started in Him. This is why the first Christians lived with such defiant joy under empires and persecution. They knew the old order was passing away, and a new creation was rising in its place.

Not one corner of creation, not one inch of your life, can remain untouched by it. If Jesus rose from the dead, then a new kind of life has begun— one that death cannot touch, sin cannot own, and fear cannot contain.

And here is the mystery: in His rising, we rise. Not metaphorically. Not someday. Now. The empty tomb is not only His story—it is ours. Paul writes, *"God... made us alive together with Christ... and raised us up with Him"* (Ephesians 2:4–6). The resurrection is not an event to admire from a distance. It is a reality to participate in.

Paul's words in Romans 8, pull this revelation even wider. Creation itself, he says, is groaning like a woman in labor, yearning for the revealing of the sons and daughters of God. The resurrection isn't only about human destiny; it's about cosmic healing.

The soil, the oceans, the galaxies—all of it is drawn into the renewal Christ began that morning in the garden. Redemption is not evacuation, but restoration. The Creator has not abandoned His creation; He is redeeming it from the inside out. Every sunrise, every act of compassion, every healed relationship whispers that the groaning is giving way to glory.

That truth first broke into the world on a morning when grief was still heavy in the air.

It was just after sunrise. The sky was blushing with the faint light of dawn. Mary Magdalene walked quickly toward the tomb, her hands clutching the burial spices she never got to use. Her heart was heavy from the blur of the last few days: arrest, trial, cross, silence. The ground felt different under her feet. She told herself it was just the dew, but something else stirred that she couldn't yet name.

When she reached the tomb, the stone was gone. Not rolled halfway—gone. Her breath caught. She bent down, peered inside. Empty linen. No body.

She ran to tell Peter and John. They came, saw, and left. But Mary returned, unable to leave the place where grief and mystery collided. Tears blurred her vision as she leaned into the opening again. Two figures clothed in light sat where His body had been. "Woman, why are you weeping?"

"They have taken my Lord," she said, voice breaking, "and I don't know where they have laid Him."

She turned, and a man stood behind her. She did not recognize Him. Perhaps He was the gardener.

"Woman," He asked again, "why are you weeping? Whom are you seeking?"

Through her tears she pleaded, "If you have carried Him away, tell me where you have laid Him, and I will take Him."

Then: one word.

"Mary."

It was His voice. The air changed. Her knees gave way. "Rabboni!" she cried, reaching for Him. But He gently steadied her. *"Do not cling to Me, for I have not yet ascended to the Father. Go instead to My brothers, and tell them, 'I am ascending to My Father and your Father, to My God and your God.'"*

Her grief turned into mission. The revolution had begun, and she was the first one sent.

The resurrection is not God hitting "undo" on death. It is the dawn of a life death cannot touch. It is the first eruption of God's new creation in the middle of the old one. The revolution started with an empty tomb, and the sound of your name on His lips.

To see the resurrection is to know that the powers of sin, death, and fear have lost their final word. To live in the resurrection is to live as if that is true, because it is.

Resurrection living looks like joy in hardship, because no loss is final. It looks like courage in risk, because even if you fall, you will rise again. It looks like peacemaking in conflict, because reconciliation is the destiny of all things in Christ.

Resurrection is not private optimism; it's a divine protest. It refuses to accept that violence, corruption, and despair will have the last word. As modern theologian N.T. Wright points out, the resurrection of Jesus was God's "Yes" to creation and His "No" to every power that distorts it. When believers forgive in the face of betrayal, when communities rebuild after devastation, when hope rises in impossible places: resurrection continues. It is the Spirit's rebellion against resignation. To live resurrected is to stand in defiance of every narrative that says things will never change, and to embody the one that already has. It is not escapism, as though resurrection only matters for the afterlife. It is not denial, as though wounds and scars vanish overnight. Jesus rose with His scars still visible. Resurrection does not erase reality. It transforms it.

The tomb is empty, and so is your old self. You rise in His rising, not someday, but now. You are not waiting for new life to begin. You are learning to walk in the life that has already begun.

The revolution has started. It is personal. It is cosmic. And it is yours.

Chapter Eight
What Must I Do to Be Saved?

I t is one of the most famous questions in the Bible, and perhaps one of the most misunderstood: *"What must I do to be saved?"*

For many, the answer has been framed as a formula: pray this prayer, repeat these words, walk this aisle, sign this card. If you do it right and mean it enough, God will forgive you and you'll be in.

But Scripture gives us another picture entirely.

Salvation is not something we initiate. It is not us getting God's attention or convincing Him to love us. It is awakening to what has already been done: to the life Christ has already given, the inclusion He has already declared, the embrace He has never withdrawn.

This is what we see in Acts 16.

An earthquake shakes the prison where Paul and Silas are held. Doors fly open. Chains fall loose. In the chaos, a Philippian jailer—responsible for the prisoners' lives—assumes the worst. Roman law says his own life is forfeit, if even one man escapes. Despair grips him. He draws his sword to end it.

But before he can act, Paul's voice cuts through the dust and darkness: *Do yourself no harm! We are all here!"*

For a moment the air itself trembles—dust settling, hearts pounding. What just happened in that cell is more than a jailbreak; it's a revelation. Grace has broken the rules. The man who thought death was his only escape, is about to find life waiting in the rubble. The same power that shook the foundations of the prison has reached for the foundations of his soul.

The jailer freezes. This is not what he expected. He rushes into the cell block, trembling. These men, who had been singing hymns through the night, have no interest in running. Something in them is freer than what any earthquake, opportunity, or open door could give.

He falls before Paul and Silas, and asks the only question that makes sense in a moment like this: *"Sirs, what must I do to be saved?"*

The jailer was not asking how to avoid hell or earn heaven. He was witnessing a different kind of kingdom: a kingdom where peace holds in the face of danger, where love refuses to abandon even when freedom is within reach.

Paul's answer is breathtaking in its simplicity: *"Believe in the Lord Jesus, and you will be saved, you and your household"* (Acts 16:31). Not "perform." Not "prove yourself." Not "get everything right first." Just believe. Trust. Surrender to the reality of who Jesus is and what He has already done.

This is where clarity matters. To say we are "already included" in Christ does not mean everyone automatically lives in the joy of salvation without faith or consent. It means that, objectively, Christ has reconciled all things to Himself (Colossians 1:20). Subjectively, we still respond: awakening to that reality, receiving it, participating in it.

"Faith is not the price of admission. It is the opening of the eyes."

For the first followers of Jesus, salvation was never a slogan or a transaction: it was a shared life. When they gathered, they weren't performing religion; they were awakening to reality. In baptism's waters and the breaking of bread, they celebrated the life they already possessed in Christ. These moments didn't *create* union; they *revealed* it. The word they used for salvation—*sozo*—meant healing, restoration, wholeness. To be saved was to be brought into harmony with God and with one another, to live from the wholeness that grace had already accomplished. Every act of mercy, every table opened to a stranger, every injustice confronted was a living picture of the gospel. Salvation was not escape from the world, but the healing of it.

Salvation is not God finally deciding you belong. It is you finally deciding to believe Him. To believe is to wake up inside a love that was there all along. It is less a decision of the mind than a surrender of the heart: a quiet yes to the grace that has been calling your name. When Jesus told Nicodemus that he must be "born again," He was not prescribing a ritual, but describing a rebirth of awareness. Salvation feels like light flooding a dark room, like lungs remembering how to breathe. You begin to realize that faith is not the ladder you climb to reach God; it's the rest you enter when you discover He's already here. And when you believe, something shifts. Fear begins to lose its grip. Guilt no longer drives you; grace begins to lead you. You stop relating to God as a distant judge you must appease and start walking with Him as a Father who shares His life with you.

Living as one already loved means your prayers are not auditions: they are conversations. Your forgiveness toward others is not a reluctant obligation; it is the overflow of the forgiveness you have received. Your hope is not fragile; it is rooted in the unshakable "yes" God has already spoken over you in Christ. That "yes" was determined before the beginning began—before you ever took your first breath.

Grace is not waiting to be summoned. It has been running toward you all along.

When salvation takes hold, it shows. Not in perfection or pretense, but in presence. Love starts finding its way into the smallest corners of a life: how we speak, how we forgive, how we see one another. The gospel is not proven by arguments; it is embodied in awakened people. Paul once said that the kingdom is "righteousness, peace, and joy in the Holy Spirit," and that is what begins to bloom in those who finally believe. It's the slow miracle of a life becoming whole. Grace does what law never could: it teaches the heart to beat in rhythm with God's own.

The jailer that night did not sign a card or memorize a script. He stepped into the reality of what was already true: that God, in Christ, had come for him. And when he did, everything changed, not only for him, but for his whole household.

Salvation is the great awakening. And when your eyes open, you see what has always been waiting for you: the God who has only ever been for you.

Chapter Nine
Born Again, Again

I t was late when he came.

The streets of Jerusalem had gone quiet, though a faint hum still lingered from the day's bustle. Nicodemus moved quickly, his cloak pulled close, eyes scanning the shadows. He was a respected Pharisee, a teacher of Israel, a man accustomed to public honor, yet here he was, slipping through the night to find Jesus.

He found Him alone, perhaps on a rooftop where the cool breeze cut through the day's heat. Oil lamps cast a soft glow, just enough to see the contours of His face. Nicodemus cleared his throat, beginning with flattery: *"Rabbi, we know You are a teacher come from God."*

But Jesus didn't wait for the speech to unfold.

"Unless one is born again, he cannot see the kingdom of God."

The words landed like a riddle. Born again? Nicodemus' mind went literal: rebirth, the womb, the impossibility of it all. Jesus' gaze was steady, His tone more invitation than argument.

> *"That which is born of the flesh is flesh, and that which is born of the Spirit is spirit. Do not marvel that I said to you, 'You must be born again.' The wind blows where it wishes... so it is with everyone born of the Spirit"* (John 3:6–8).

Nicodemus was not puzzled because the idea was new, but because Jesus used familiar words in an unfamiliar way. Among the rabbis, *new birth* already described what happened when Gentiles converted to Israel's faith or when a fallen Israelite was restored to covenant life. It meant re-entry into

God's family, a kind of fresh beginning. Jesus took that ancient hope and widened it: this rebirth would not come through ritual or status but through the Spirit Himself: God breathing His own life into humanity. To be born from above is to discover that heaven's life has entered earth's story, and you are part of it.

Nicodemus had devoted his life to religion, study, and discipline. Yet Jesus spoke as if the life he longed for was not achieved by effort, but awakened by the Spirit, as if it had been waiting for him all along.

That is the thing about new birth. It is not a second attempt at the life you've been living. It is a revelation of the life you were made for. It is not starting over from scratch. It is waking up to the reality that, in Christ, your truest life has always been held secure.

Yet even after the first awakening, life has a way of covering what grace has revealed. That's why the Spirit keeps returning: not as a one-time spark but as the steady rhythm of resurrection. Paul wrote that we are "raised with Christ" so that we might *walk* in newness of life, not simply remember it (Romans 6:4). Every time you forgive, risk love, or let an old version of yourself die, resurrection happens again. The same Spirit who hovered over the waters in Genesis now hovers over the fragments of your story, shaping new creation within you.

This moment ties together Genesis and resurrection, creation and redemption. The same breath that spoke light into the void is the breath now moving through your spirit. The first creation began with "Let there be"; the new creation begins with "It is finished." To be born again is to live in that divine overlap—heaven's life flooding earth's story through you. The Spirit does not discard what you've been; He resurrects it. Every redeemed fragment becomes part of God's masterpiece of restoration.

Being born again was never meant to be a single event on your timeline; it is the ongoing miracle of God's breath restoring what fear and failure tried to bury. And that's the mystery of salvation: it keeps unfolding.

Union with God does not begin at the moment you "get saved." It is the eternal intention of God, revealed in Christ and awakened within you by the Spirit. New birth is the Spirit pulling back the curtain on that reality and you stepping into it with open eyes.

And yet, even this awakening is not the end. The Spirit keeps teaching us to be born again—again. Every season, every surrender, every moment of rediscovery is another unfolding of that same grace. The breath that first filled your lungs at salvation is still moving through you, calling dead places to rise. To live in Christ is to live in perpetual renewal. The soul that once strained to reach God now learns to rest in the God who keeps reaching for you. New birth is not the doorway you once passed through; it's the air you now breathe.

But life has a way of burying that first awakening. Religion can harden it into memory. Fear can smother it. Pain can cause you to doubt it ever happened. Which is why the invitation to be "born again" is not a one-time event. You can be born again… again. And again.

Every fresh encounter with His love is another breath of new life. Every moment you turn toward Him and remember who you are in Him is another birth. This is not religious reform or moral self-improvement. It is the Spirit doing what only the Spirit can do: breathing life into what has grown still.

Ezekiel saw it centuries earlier: God promising a new heart, a new spirit, and breath filling dry bones until they rose as a living army (Ezekiel 36–37). Jesus was fulfilling that promise in real time, with Nicodemus that night, and with us now.

You will find that this cycle of rebirth does not grow easier, but it does grow deeper. Each new beginning asks for a little more surrender, a little more trust. But it also reveals a greater tenderness in God than you have ever known. There is no limit to how many times you can start over in grace. The Kingdom is built on this rhythm: death and life, falling and rising, letting go and receiving again. To be born again, again, is to live unafraid of the unfinished places, knowing that the Spirit who began a good work will not stop until all things are made new.

So what does it mean to be born again... again? It might look like compassion rising where cynicism once lived. It might look like forgiveness loosening the grip of an old wound. It might look like joy welling up in you simply because you are with Him.

To be born again is not to become someone else. It is to finally see yourself—your true self—in the light of God's love. And every breath you take in His Spirit is another beginning, another mercy, another reminder that you were made alive in Him long before you knew His name. Like Nicodemus under the night sky, you stand where mystery meets mercy.

You can begin again. Right now.

The Spirit is not finished with you.

The wind still blows, even in the dark.

The invitation is still on the table, no matter how long it has been.

So lift your head. Breathe deep. Step forward.

This is your moment to rise into the life that has always been yours in Christ. And nothing—not your past, not your failures, not even your doubt—can keep you from being born again... again.

Chapter Ten
The Gospel for the Religious

The night air pulsed with music and laughter. Tambourines echoed from the courtyard. The scent of roasted meat drifted into the fields. The ground itself seemed to vibrate beneath the rhythm of dancing feet. Inside the house, servants moved quickly, pouring wine and carrying platters piled high. The celebration had begun, and the whole village knew why.

But outside, just beyond the light spilling from the doorway, the elder brother stood still. His arms were crossed tight across his chest. His jaw was set. Every step toward the party felt like surrender to something he could not understand: a grace that offended his sense of fairness.

The father saw him standing there. He left the feast and came into the dark to meet him. You can almost hear the weariness in his voice, not from frustration but from longing:

"Son, you are always with me, and everything I have is yours. But we had to celebrate and be glad, because your brother… he was dead and is alive again; he was lost and is found" (Luke 15:31–32).

It is one of the most tender moments in Scripture—not a lecture, not a rebuke, but an invitation. Yet the parable ends without telling us if the elder brother ever stepped inside.

Many of us know that feeling all too well. We've served faithfully, kept the rules, given generously, and done all the "right" things. We've shown up early, stayed late, filled every slot on the volunteer schedule. We know the lyrics to every song and the right answer to every Bible study question. And somewhere along the way, without even noticing, we began to measure our worth by what we could do for God rather than who we are to Him (Ephesians 2:8–9).

This is the quiet danger of the religious mindset. It builds identity on what you can earn, all while standing in the middle of an inheritance you never paid for.

The father's words to the elder brother are just as true for us: *"You are always with Me, and everything I have is yours"*(Luke 15:31). When we forget this, or fail to recognize it, we slip into religious striving. It is not open rebellion, but quiet barrenness of heart. It is serving without joy. It is living in the house without joining the party.

In modern terms, it looks like defining your spirituality by ministry output. Feeling threatened when grace reaches someone you think hasn't "earned it." Being more comfortable with duty than with delight. Resisting joy because it feels unspiritual.

This is not about abandoning faithfulness or discipline. It is about remembering that faithfulness is meant to flow from belovedness, not insecurity (John 15:9–11). If obedience is fueled by fear, suspicion, or comparison, then we are no closer to the Father's heart than the prodigal was in the pigpen.

The Gospel is for the religious too. It is for the faithful servant who forgot he was a son. It is for the worship leader who hasn't enjoyed worship in years. It is for the small group leader who quietly resents the people they serve. It is for anyone so busy working for God that they have forgotten how to sit with Him.

You do not have to earn a seat at the feast. The table was set with you in mind before you ever took your first step toward the house. And the Father is still coming outside, still speaking your name, still saying, *"Everything I have is yours."*

The question is the same now as it was that night: Will you come in?

Chapter Eleven
The Gospel for the Wounded

Dust swirled at ankle height as worshipers moved toward the temple, unaware that a storm of accusation was about to break. The morning light was bright, but the atmosphere was heavy. A crowd pressed in, their voices sharp and urgent, dragging a woman forward like evidence in a trial. She stumbled, her shame laid bare before men who saw her as nothing more than a lesson to be made. Her hair tangled, her clothes disheveled, arms clinging to herself as if she could hold her dignity together.

In the center stood Jesus, calm yet unflinching, His posture a quiet defiance against the chaos about to unfold.

"They caught her in the act," someone hissed. The words moved through the crowd like venom.

The men pushing her forward quoted the Law of Moses—cold, sharp, unquestionable. The penalty was clear: death by stoning. But this was about more than her. They wanted to test Jesus, to trap Him, to force Him to choose between upholding the law and showing compassion.

They demanded an answer. But Jesus did not match their urgency. He did not fire back an argument. He knelt. The hem of His robe brushed the dust as He wrote on the ground with His finger. No one knows what He wrote. Perhaps their names. Perhaps the sins they thought no one saw. Perhaps nothing more than lines in the dirt: a reminder that every accusation eventually blows away.

The crowd pressed harder. The tension thickened. She braced herself for the first stone.

Then He stood. His eyes swept over the mob: not with fear, not with disgust, but with piercing truth.

"Let the one who is without sin throw the first stone."

Silence.

One by one, the stones dropped. The oldest left first. Then the younger ones. Soon only the woman remained, her breath uneven, her heart pounding.

Jesus met her eyes.
"Where are your accusers?"
She looked around. "No one, Lord."
"Then neither do I condemn you," He said. "Go, and from now on, sin no more" (John 8:2–11).

In that moment, she was safer than she had ever been, not because her past had been erased, but because she had been fully seen and still chosen.

Many who have been wounded by religion have never stood in a place like that with Jesus. Instead, they have stood in rooms filled with accusation. They have sat across from leaders who twisted Scripture into a weapon. They have heard the sharp edge of judgment and the cold silence of withdrawal.

And here is the truth you must know: what hurt you was not the heart of God. The rejection, the shame, the manipulation, the neglect: none of it bore His image. Jesus does not gaslight the wounded. He does not minimize their pain. He does not dismiss their grief as oversensitivity. He looks you in the eye and names the wrong, then offers a grace that heals without excusing.

Grace never demands that you pretend you were not hurt. It does not rush your recovery or shame you for bleeding too long. The gospel is not a pep talk that says "get over it," but a Presence that whispers, "I'm staying." Jesus does not heal by erasing what happened; He heals by re-narrating it in light of His love. In trauma, the body remembers what safety forgot. But when grace enters, memory begins to breathe again. Slowly, the nervous system learns peace. The heart relearns trust. The soul begins to believe that gentleness is not a trap. The miracle of healing is not forgetting; it is remembering differently: seeing your story now held inside His.

The church may have misrepresented Him. People may have misused His name. But His character is not up for revision. He is the same yesterday, today, and forever. The same Jesus who shielded the woman in the courtyard shields you still.

"To be wounded is not to be disqualified. Your doubt does not scare Him. Your anger does not make Him flinch. Your mistrust is not a dealbreaker."

Eight days after His resurrection, another wounded soul stood before Him.

Thomas had missed the first gathering when Jesus appeared to His disciples. He had heard the others' breathless reports: *"We've seen the Lord!"* But something in him ached too deeply to receive it. He could not bring himself to hope again.

"I will not believe unless I see the nail marks in His hands," he said. "Unless I put my finger where the nails were and place my hand in His side."

It was not cynicism. It was grief. It was the defense mechanism of someone who had trusted once and been devastated.

A week later, the room was full again. The door was locked. Fear still clung to them. Then suddenly, Jesus was there. No knock. No warning. Just presence.

"Peace be with you."

Then He turned directly to Thomas. He did not scold him. He did not make him feel small. He invited him close: *"Put your finger here. See My hands. Reach out your hand and put it into My side. Stop doubting and believe."*

Thomas's knees may have buckled as his defenses collapsed in a flood of recognition. *"My Lord and my God!"* (John 20:24–29).

Jesus met Thomas exactly where his wound demanded. He did not shame him for needing proof. He provided it. To be wounded is not to be disqualified. Your doubt does not scare Him. Your anger does not make Him flinch. Your mistrust is not a dealbreaker. Every wound you carry is seen, and none of them have ever made you less His.

The risen Christ did not hide His scars. He held them out like invitations. The proof of His divinity was not the absence of pain, but the redemption of it. When Thomas touched those wounds, he was really touching his own—the despair of dreams deferred, the ache of unanswered prayers, the grief of unmet expectations.

Every believer who encounters the risen Jesus discovers the same truth: the wounds of Christ are not reminders of failure but doors into empathy. They tell us that God has entered the human story so completely that even our suffering is not foreign to Him. This is why healing in His presence never feels like dismissal. It feels like recognition. He knows. He's been there. And somehow, because He still bears His scars, yours can become places where light breaks through.

And if you have been hurt in His name, hear this: you do not have to shrink back from His gaze. His eyes are the one place where your scars are not met with suspicion.

Healing may not happen overnight, but it is possible. Begin here: slow down. Give yourself permission to rest from religious performance. Healing often comes in the pause. Listen in prayer. Let it be less about speaking and more about hearing His voice whisper, *"I am here."* Find safe community: people who reflect His gentleness and truth, who can walk with you without agenda.

The woman in the courtyard walked away forgiven and free. Thomas walked away believing again. Both walked away whole, not because they had avoided pain, but because Jesus met them there. He has not changed. The Gospel for the wounded is this: you are safe with Him. Always.

Chapter Twelve
The Gospel for the World

From the crowded streets of Jerusalem to the distant coastlines of every continent, the Gospel has been moving like wind across the ages. It has crossed borders, broken language barriers, and taken root in places no one thought it could grow. Empires have risen and fallen, yet its story has never slowed. From whispered prayers in underground churches to songs in open-air markets, from baptismal waters in quiet villages to the bustling noise of city streets, the news has spread: God's love is not a local rumor. It is the headline of the universe.

"For God so loved the world..." These words are so familiar that they risk sounding small —too often recited, seldom realized— as if "the world" were just a collection of individuals needing rescue from hell. But in John 3:16, "world" means *cosmos*: everything God made, every corner of creation. It means people, yes, but also systems, cultures, ecosystems, languages, economies, and histories. The scope is staggering. God is not merely collecting souls; He is reconciling all things to Himself.

When John used the word *kosmos*, he meant more than the sum of human souls—he meant every atom, every system, every unseen pattern that holds creation together. The love of God is not just sentimental; it is structural. It moves through ecosystems and economies, through culture and consciousness, restoring what fragmentation has stolen. Paul echoed this when he wrote that through Christ, God was pleased "to reconcile all things, whether on earth or in heaven" (Colossians 1:20). The Cross reached as far as the curse. In that single act of self-giving love, heaven and earth were restitched at the torn seam. The Gospel, then, is not about escape but restoration: God setting creation back into rhythm with Himself until every molecule hums again with grace.

This is why resurrection matters for the world. The empty tomb was not the end of Jesus' personal story. It was the first page of a new world breaking in. In His rising, God declared that death would not have the last word over creation. The resurrection was the dawn of new creation—a reality in which justice, peace, healing, and joy are no longer wishful thinking but inevitable outcomes of His reign.

When you see the Gospel this way, it cannot be reduced to private morality or church attendance. It sends you into the world with a new posture. You are not escaping the world; you are participating in its renewal.

You become a peacemaker in divided spaces, a voice for the marginalized, a restorer of broken relationships, a caretaker of the earth. The Gospel invites you to see every act of mercy, every word of truth, and every work of justice as part of God's cosmic mission.

Pentecost is our proof that this mission is not limited by geography or culture. On that day, Jerusalem was crowded with pilgrims from "every nation under heaven" (Acts 2:5). The morning air buzzed with a hundred languages, the clamor of trade, the shuffle of feet in narrow streets. Then came the sound, like a mighty rushing wind, filling the house where the disciples waited. Flames rested on each of them, and suddenly the Good News spilled out in every language represented in the crowd. Parthians heard it in theirs. Egyptians in theirs. Romans in theirs. What religion had divided, the Spirit was uniting in sound: It was as if God Himself were saying, *"No culture is left out. No voice is too foreign. My Spirit speaks your language."*

That day, the Gospel leapt from a small upper room into the bloodstream of the world. It has never retreated. It moves still: through you, through us, through the Church that remembers it is more than a weekly gathering.

So lift your eyes beyond the borders of your own life. See the Gospel already advancing in refugee camps and city councils, in the patient work of reconciliation and the fierce fight for justice, in quiet acts of compassion and bold public witness. The Kingdom is not retreating. It is increasing. Its government and peace will know no end. Every day, another corner of creation is lit with the knowledge of the glory of the Lord, until the whole earth shines with it.

The Gospel refuses to stay confined to personal spirituality. It breathes through policies and art, through science and soil, through every place where God's image is waiting to be recognized again. When we advocate for justice, care for creation, or speak peace into violence, we are not doing "extra" work beyond the Gospel: we are living it. Redemption touches rivers and neighborhoods alike.

The Spirit who hovered over the waters in Genesis now hovers over cities, waiting for sons and daughters to speak light once more. To follow Jesus is to collaborate with that hovering: to plant gardens in deserts, to mend what empire breaks, to believe that love can rewrite the story of nations as surely as it rewrote ours.

We are not waiting for the world to be redeemed; we are walking with the Redeemer Himself, carrying resurrection in our breath and the atmosphere of heaven in our steps.

Chapter Thirteen
The Table Is Still Set

The smell of fresh bread mingles with the sweetness of fruit and the savory richness of roasted lamb. Candlelight flickers against polished wood. A low hum of laughter and quiet conversation fills the air. Every place at the long table is prepared: cups waiting to be filled, plates ready for abundance. The Host's chair is not empty. He is here. His eyes search for yours. His smile is not the polite kind you offer a stranger, but the warmth of a friend who has been expecting you.

This table is not an invention of church tradition or religious imagination. It is as old as the garden, when God walked with humanity in the cool of the day. It is as present as the meal Jesus shared with His friends the night before His crucifixion. And it is as future as the marriage supper of the Lamb, when heaven and earth are made one. The table is the picture of what God has always wanted: unbroken communion.

The Emmaus Table

Two men trudged down a dusty road, the late-afternoon sun stretching their shadows ahead of them. Passover was over, but their hearts were anything but full. Grief clung like a heavy cloak. The Teacher they had followed was dead. Their hope was buried in the same tomb that now lay empty, though they could not bring themselves to believe the rumors of resurrection.

A stranger joined them, matching their pace. His voice was calm, curious. "What are you discussing?" he asked. They poured out the story: the betrayal, the trial, the cross. The stranger listened, then began to speak of Moses and the prophets, weaving a story that made their hearts burn, though they did not yet know why.

When evening came, they urged Him to stay. At the table, the stranger took bread, gave thanks, broke it, and placed it in their hands. In that moment, the shadows fell away. Light flooded their understanding. This was no stranger. It was Jesus. He had been with them the whole time. Before they could speak, He vanished, but the bread still rested in their hands, and their hearts burned brighter than the candles on the table.

The table does not only feed you. It opens your eyes to the One who has been walking with you all along (Luke 24:13–35).

Breakfast on the Shore

It was early morning on the Sea of Galilee. A gray mist floated above the water as the disciples dragged in an empty net for the third time that night. No fish. No catch. Just weariness and the ache of failure.

Then a voice called from the shore, "Friends, have you any fish?" They answered no. "Throw your net on the right side of the boat," He said. The net filled instantly, straining under the weight. John's eyes widened. "It's the Lord!"

Peter did not wait for the boat. He threw himself into the water, wading and stumbling toward the figure on the beach. A charcoal fire crackled. Bread and fish were already roasting. Jesus looked up and smiled. "Come and have breakfast."

They ate in silence, the sound of waves and fire filling the space between them. Then Jesus turned to Peter, the one who had denied Him three times, and asked, "Do you love Me?" Three times the question. Three times the affirmation. Three times the restoration. The smell of another charcoal fire, the one in the high priest's courtyard, was replaced by the aroma of breakfast with the risen Lord.

The Host was still serving, still restoring, still making room (John 21:1–19).

The Invitation Remains

The table is still set. Not because you remembered to come, but because the Host has never left. The candles still burn. The bread is still warm. The cup still overflows. A place here has always borne your name.

This table is for the honest: whether your honesty sounds like worship or like a weary sigh. It is for the hungry: whether you crave mercy's taste or the relief of being known. It is for those who never left and those who took the long way home.

"The table is still set. Not because you remembered to come, but because the Host has never left."

You do not have to prove you deserve this seat. You do not have to apologize for the delay. The One who calls you here is not tallying your absences. He is lifting His eyes at the sound of your footsteps and smiling as if you never left.

And the beauty of this table is that it does not vanish when you leave the sanctuary. It is spread across the kitchen counter when you make coffee before sunrise. It is in the whispered prayer in the car, the shared meal with a neighbor, the quiet moment when you realize you are not alone. This table is both eternal and immediate: a taste of the kingdom to come, breaking into the kingdom now.

So come. Come as you are, and keep coming. The table is not just set for you. It is set with you in mind. And as long as the King is on the throne, the invitation remains.

A Final Word

Before you ever reached for Him, He had already reached for you. Before your first prayer, your first song, your first tear—His voice had already named you beloved. You were His before you knew His name. You are His now. You will be His forever.

Every chapter of this book has been another way of telling you the same thing: God is like Jesus. There has never been a day when He was not with you. There has never been a moment when you were outside His presence, His care, or His heart. The Cross did not convince Him to love you. It convinced you.

You are not on the outside looking in. You are already at the table, the place prepared for you before time began. You are not lost in the crowd; you are in the center of His gaze. No failure, no wound, no detour has ever removed you from His arms.

So breathe. Let your shoulders drop. Let your heart slow its anxious beating. You are home. You are safe. Receive His joy. Receive His grace. Receive His peace. And rest assured that He has received you.

When you rise from these pages and step back into your world, carry this truth like breath in your lungs: you are seen. You are cared for. You are loved —forever and always.

This is the Gospel.

Acknowledgments

To my family: thank you. Every chapter of my life has been shaped by your love, and every word of this book carries your imprint. To my parents, Rev. Dr. James and Rev. Ericka Bailey, your love has been a mirror of God's heart. You have walked with me, believed in me, and covered me. What you have poured into me will echo through generations.

To every person I have encountered along the way: this work is for you. Your lives, your questions, your stories, your joy, and your pain have helped shape the message within these pages. You have reminded me that theology must be lived, and that the Gospel shines brightest when it meets people in the grit of real life.

To the readers, especially those who wrestled through this book with open hearts, thank you for your courage. Thank you for leaning in when it would have been easier to turn away. Thank you for daring to believe that maybe, just maybe, God is better than we were told.

I honor the life and legacy of Archbishop Veron Ashe. His ministry opened a gateway into the wider possibilities of God. His voice assured me that I was not alone and that there truly is more.

Above all, to the God who is greater, kinder, and more loving than I ever could have imagined, I count it an honor to share Your love and proclaim Your glorious Gospel. May I spend my life doing so.

Recommended Reading

The Gospel is not a finish line—it is an open door into the eternal heart of God. These voices, books, and ministries have helped me see Jesus more clearly, understand Scripture more deeply, and walk more fully in the grace of union and identity. I offer them to you as companions for the journey—trusted guides for those awakening to the love that has always held us.

Foundational Books & Authors:

Myths and Mistranslations by Jamie Englehart
A powerful dismantling of seventy commonly misunderstood Scriptures, offering clarity, context, and grace.

The Gospel for Christians by Howard J. Grimes
A tender, truth-filled reintroduction to the Gospel, especially for those wounded by religion.

The Shack by William Paul Young
A story of divine healing that invites readers into the mystery of God's relational love.

Jesus and the Undoing of Adam and **The Great Dance** by C. Baxter Kruger

Deep yet accessible explorations of the finished work of Christ, our inclusion in the Trinity, and the truth of union.

On the Incarnation by St. Athanasius

An early Church Father's powerful testimony to the purpose and glory of the Incarnation.

Mystical Union by John Crowder

A jubilant, Spirit-drenched declaration of the believer's union with Christ.

Simply Jesus, Surprised by Hope, and **The Day the Revolution Began** by N.T. Wright

Reframes the Gospel in its first-century Jewish context and recovers its power as a story of resurrection and new creation.

Understanding the Bible Through the Eyes of a Hebrew by Shane Willard

Restores the original worldview of Scripture and brings fresh insight to Jesus' teachings.

Let this Gospel carry you—not just to deeper belief, but to deeper being. Keep listening. Keep beholding. Keep unlearning what love never said. You are included, you are seen, and you are safe in Him.

The journey continues.

Glossary

Alienation (ay-lee-uh-NAY-shun)
The condition of feeling separated from God, though in truth that separation exists only in our minds. The Cross reveals that God never withdrew His presence —He has always been near, drawing us back into awareness of union.

Athanasius (ath-uh-NAY-shus)
A fourth-century Church Father best known for *On the Incarnation*, where he taught that the Son of God became human so that humanity might share in divine life.

Belovedness (bih-LUHV-id-ness)
The unchanging state of being perfectly loved and accepted by God. Belovedness is not achieved; it is recognized.

Covenant (KUHV-uh-nuhnt)
God's enduring commitment of love toward humanity. In Christ, covenant is not a contract of

performance but a relationship of participation—
God binding Himself to us in faithfulness and grace.

Divine Participation (dih-VYN par-tis-uh-PAY-shun)
The shared life of God and humanity through Christ
and the Spirit. Salvation is not escape from the world
but entrance into God's own fellowship.

Glory (GLOR-ee)
The radiant expression of God's nature—love made
visible. In Jesus, glory is not power displayed over
others but self-giving presence revealed for others.

Gregory of Nyssa (GREG-uh-ree uhv NISS-uh)
A fourth-century theologian and mystic who taught
that humanity's journey with God is one of continual
transformation into divine likeness.

Holy Imagination (HOH-lee ih-MAJ-uh-nay-shun)
The Spirit-illumined ability to perceive reality
through the lens of grace. Holy imagination allows
us to see the world as God sees it—beloved and
being made whole.

Inclusion (in-KLOO-zhun)
The truth that all humanity has been gathered into Christ's reconciling work. No one stands outside the reach of divine embrace.

Incarnation (in-kar-NAY-shun)
The mystery of God becoming human in Jesus Christ. In the Incarnation, divinity and humanity meet without separation, revealing God's nearness and our true worth.

Irenaeus (ear-uh-NAY-us)
A second-century bishop who taught that Christ recapitulates—or re-lives—every stage of human existence to heal and restore it. His vision shaped much of early Christian theology.

Justice (Restorative) (JUHS-tis reh-STOR-uh-tiv)
The justice of God that makes things right by healing, not harming; by restoring relationship rather than demanding retribution.

Kenosis (keh-NOH-sis)
From the Greek for "emptying." Refers to Christ's

self-giving humility in taking on human form—love that pours itself out for the sake of others.

Metanoia (met-uh-NOY-uh)
A Greek word often translated "repentance." It means a change of mind—a turning from illusion to truth, from fear to love.

Ontology / Ontological (on-TAH-luh-jee / on-tuh-LAH-juh-kul)
From the Greek *ontos*, meaning "being." To speak of ontological union is to affirm that our very existence is sustained in God; we were never truly separate from Him in being, only in perception.

Perichoresis (peh-ri-ko-REE-sis)
The divine dance of mutual indwelling between Father, Son, and Spirit. Each fully lives in the other, and through Christ, we are invited into that same communion.

Presence (PREZ-uhns)
The active nearness of God that fills all creation. Awareness of the Presence is the birthplace of worship, peace, and transformation.

Recapitulation (ree-kuh-PIT-yuh-lay-shun)
The early Christian teaching that Jesus re-lived the human story from birth to death, redeeming every stage of our existence and restoring creation's intended harmony.

Reconciliation (rek-uhn-SIL-ee-ay-shun)
God's act of bringing humanity and creation back into harmony with Himself—not through appeasement but through the revelation of unbreakable love.

Sozo (SOH-zo)
A Greek word meaning "to save," encompassing healing, deliverance, protection, and wholeness. Salvation in Scripture is total restoration—spirit, soul, and body.

Tabernacle (TAB-ur-na-kul)
The portable dwelling place of God's presence among Israel. It foreshadows the reality revealed in Christ—God choosing to dwell within humanity.

Tertullian (tur-TUL-ee-un)
An early North-African theologian (second–third

century) who coined much of the language later used to describe the Trinity and the work of Christ.

Theosis (THEE-oh-sis)
The participation of humanity in God's own life—being transformed by grace into the likeness of Christ.

Trinity (TRIN-uh-tee)
The eternal communion of Father, Son, and Holy Spirit—one God in three persons, perfectly united in love. The Trinity is not a hierarchy but a relationship of mutual indwelling, revealing that the essence of God is relational love.

Trinitarian Life (trin-ih-TARE-ee-uhn lyfe)
Living from the shared love of Father, Son, and Spirit. The Christian life is not imitation from afar but participation in divine fellowship.

Union (YOO-nyun)
The central reality of the Gospel: humanity's oneness with God in Christ through the Spirit. Union is not achieved by effort but awakened by revelation—the

discovery that we have always been included in Love.

Scripture Index

Hosea 2:14–20 – God's covenant love compared to a faithful husband.
Hosea 2:14–15 – God luring His people into the wilderness to speak tenderly to them.

Daniel
Daniel 3:24–27 – God's presence with the three Hebrew boys in the fire.

Jonah
Jonah 1:17; 2:1–10 – Jonah swallowed by a great fish and crying out to God.

Isaiah
Isaiah 6:1–7 – Isaiah's vision of God's glory in the temple.
Isaiah 59:1–2 – Perceived separation from God; His arm not too short to save.

Psalm
Psalm 145:8 – The Lord is gracious and compassionate, slow to anger and rich in love.

Matthew
Matthew 14:22–33 – Peter stepping out of the boat during the storm.
Matthew 27:51 – The temple veil torn from top to bottom at Christ's death.

Mark

Mark 1:40–42 – Jesus touching and healing the leper.

Mark 1:14–15 – Jesus announcing, "The kingdom of God has come near."

Luke

Luke 1:26–38 – The angel's announcement to Mary of Jesus' birth.

Luke 6:1–7 – Jesus forgiving and cleansing Isaiah's vision. *(contextual reference)*

Luke 8:1–11 – The woman caught in adultery.

Luke 15:11–32 – The parable of the prodigal son and the elder brother.

Luke 21:1–19 – Jesus restoring Peter at the breakfast on the shore.

Luke 23:32–34 – Jesus praying, "Father, forgive them," from the Cross.

Luke 24:13–35 – The Emmaus road and breaking of bread.

John

John 1:14 – The Word became flesh.

John 1:18 – Jesus making the Father known.

John 3:1–21 – Jesus and Nicodemus on being born again.

John 4:4–42 – Jesus and the Samaritan woman at the well.

John 8:2–11 – The woman caught in adultery.

John 14:9 – Whoever has seen Me has seen the Father.

John 15:9–11 – Abiding in Christ's love as the source of joy and obedience.

John 17:22–23 – Jesus' prayer for oneness.

John 20:24–29 – Thomas touching Jesus' wounds.

John 21:1–19 – Jesus restoring Peter at the breakfast on the shore.

Acts

Acts 2:1–13 – Pentecost: the Spirit poured out and heard in many languages.

Acts 16:25–34 – Paul and Silas in prison; the Philippian jailer's conversion.

Romans

Romans 5:8–10 – God's love revealed while we were still sinners.

Romans 6:4 – Raised with Christ to walk in newness of life.

Romans 8:19 – Creation waiting for the revealing of the children of God.

Romans 12:17–21 – Living without vengeance; overcoming evil with good.

1 Corinthians

1 Corinthians 2:16 – Having the mind of Christ.

1 Corinthians 15:20 – Christ the firstfruits of the resurrection.

2 Corinthians
2 Corinthians 3:18 – Transformed into the same image we behold.
2 Corinthians 5:19 – God in Christ reconciling the world to Himself.

Galatians
Galatians 1:6–7 – Turning to a different gospel.
Galatians 2:20 – Crucified with Christ, living by His life.
Galatians 4:19 – Christ being formed in us.

Ephesians
Ephesians 1:4–5 – Chosen before the foundation of the world.
Ephesians 2:4–6 – Raised and seated with Christ.
Ephesians 5:14 – "Awake, O sleeper, and rise from the dead."

Philippians
Philippians 2:5 – Having the same mind as Christ.

Colossians
Colossians 1:20–21 – Reconciliation of all things; alienated in our minds.
Colossians 1:27 – Christ in you, the hope of glory.

Hebrews

Hebrews 1:3 – Jesus as the exact imprint of God's being.

1 John

1 John 4:8–10 – God is love, revealed in Christ.

Revelation

Revelation 13:8 – The Lamb slain from the foundation of the world.

Revelation 21:1–4 – The new creation and God dwelling with humanity.

About the Author

Aaron C. Bailey is a preacher, teacher, and guide whose life's work is to help people encounter the presence of God, awaken to their true identity, and live in the transforming reality of grace. For nearly two decades, he has served the Church faithfully, proclaiming the good news of Jesus with clarity, compassion, and conviction.

He is the Founder and Senior Leader of Remnant Chicago, a Christ-centered, presence-driven local church expression devoted to revealing Christ, awakening identity, and transforming the world. Aaron's ministry carries a passion for recovering the beauty and power of the faith given to us by Jesus and the early church — a faith rooted in truth, wonder, and the unshakable love of God.

Known for his ability to speak to both the heart and the mind, Aaron creates spaces where people are invited to be honest, encounter God deeply, and step into the fullness of who they were created to be. Whether preaching, writing, mentoring leaders, or hosting worship gatherings, he carries a voice of renewal for this generation — one marked by beauty, healing, and a vision of the Kingdom advancing without end.

You can connect with Aaron and follow his ministry at:

Instagram: **@itsmeaaronbailey**

Remnant Chicago: **@remnantchicago**

Website: **www.aaronbaileyglobal.com**

www.ingramcontent.com/pod-product-compliance
Lightning Source LLC
Chambersburg PA
CBHW031422120626
46545CB00006B/2232